Believing in Books
The Story of Lillian Smith

by

Sydell Waxman

illustrations by
Patty Gallinger
and Liz Milkau

Napoleon Publishing

Napoleon Publishing
Toronto Ontario Canada
www.napoleonpublishing.com

Le Conseil des Arts du Canada DEPUIS 1957 | The Canada Council for the Arts SINCE 1957

Napoleon Publishing gratefully acknowledges the support of the Canada Council for our publishing program.

The author gratefully acknowledges the supportof IBBY Canada for the Francis E. Russell Award which helped facilitate primary research.

Printed in Canada

National Library of Canada Cataloguing in Publication

Waxman, Sydell, date—
    Believing in Books: the story of Lillian Smith/ Sydell Waxman

(Stories of Canada)
ISBN 0-929141-77-6

    1. Smith, Lillian H. (Lillian Helena), 1887-1983. 2. Children's librarians--Canada--Biography. I. Title. II. Series: Stories of Canada (Toronto, Ont.)

Z720.S64W39 2002   020'.92   C2002-902964-3

Lillian H. Smith

Chapter One

Have you ever read a book that you couldn't put down? Have you shivered at the scary parts or laughed out loud at funny lines?

Over a hundred years ago, a child named Lillian felt this magic in books. Fairy tales like "The Red Shoes" danced in her mind's eye. Storms at sea sent her shivering under the covers. She hugged *Gulliver's Travels*.

As she grew older, she was troubled to learn that most children had never heard of Gulliver. Most children in the late 1800s had never trembled at the sight of Long John Silver in *Treasure Island*. They had missed tumbling down the rabbit's hole with *Alice in Wonderland*. Most children lived lives without books.

Lillian yearned to share her delight of these magical experiences. When she grew up, she struggled to place a good book into the hands and hearts of children everywhere...and she did.

Most of the libraries you visit, most of the librarians who work there, exist in Lillian's "Forest of Firsts", a realm filled with "trees" of her new ideas.

How did she convince people that stories for the young could change the world? Who was this special person whose soft voice carried this loud message? How did she start a revolution for children's books?

THE GREATEST

"...she {Lillian H. Smith} made a larger contribution to the personal enjoyment of more human beings than any other Canadian. Several generations are unaware that she was the greatest children's librarian of the century."

-Douglas Fisher, newspaper journalist

NO CHILDREN ALLOWED

Libraries, as we know them, did not exist in the late 1800s. Wealthy households and private clubs had reading rooms, but the sign often said, "No children or dogs allowed."

Favourite Room

Lillian Smith as a baby

Music and books surrounded Lillian from the day she was born on March 17, 1887, in London Ontario. Her mother Elizabeth's piano music, with its religious and classical themes, drifted through their large Victorian home. Her father John Vipond Smith, a Methodist minister and scholar, never tired of discussing English literature. Before she could decipher the alphabet, Lillian savoured the sight of beautiful books, neatly aligned in her father's library. In this special room, filled with the warm smells of oak, paper and leather, she felt the comfort of home.

Lillian's three older siblings, Arthur, Kathrina and Edna, all became willing readers. Shy Edna would curl up with Lillian at bedtime to share *Household Stories* by the Grimm Brothers. Over and over they enjoyed the tale of Grethel, the hungry cook. Lillian laughed every time Grethel ate the meal meant for company.

Eventually, Lillian pulled down *Gulliver's Travels*, opened the gold-embossed cover and read the entire story herself. Gulliver's triumphs made her heart race as though she were actually in the story. She responded so

MAGIC

"For there is magic in the writing of these books; a magic that enchants the children who read them..."
-Lillian Smith

strongly to fictional villains that she left the books outside her bedroom at night. During the day, she slipped behind the tapestry curtains so no one could see her cry through sad stories.

Elizabeth's music helped Lillian respond to the rhythmic sounds in well-crafted prose, but the love of the printed word belonged to her father. Admiring him, she grew to share his interests and traits. Like him, she developed a keen mind, strong speaking skills and an overwhelming fascination with ideas and books.

Pack It Up

An illustration from "Clever Grethel", one of Lillian's favourite stories from Grimm's *Household Stories*, illustrated in 1882 by Walter Crane.

Lillian's book characters followed her wherever she went. Each time her father received a new Canadian parish, the family had to move. Everyone helped. Lillian, the youngest, packed the treasured books.

In the new house, Lillian carefully placed her "friends" onto the dim shelves of the family library. Echoes of her mother's poetic tunes soon wafted to the images of the stories. This special room, once again, became familiar and comforting.

Even with flickering candles and the new kerosene lamps, the library was often dark. Lillian searched for well-lit private reading spots.

One day she realized that she could take her reading into the sunlight by crawling out one of the upper windows. She plunked down onto their rooftop where no one would bother her. Immersed in the make-believe land of Lilliput, she didn't notice the prickling wood shingles beneath her, or the motion as she started to slip downwards. Startled, she tried to grip the roof. Too late. Her book flew out of control, spiralling over the edge. Blue sky and green grass blurred. The roof edge whizzed by. With a thud, she slammed onto the ground. Alarmed, Elizabeth and Edna came running.

The doctor arrived by horse and buggy. He took off his tall top hat under which many doctors hid their stethoscope. He opened his

A NEW IDEA

In 1731, Benjamin Franklin was the first to allow the public lending of books. He only had 35 books, but his library soon grew to 375 books.

"FREE BOOKS FOR EVERYONE!"

Although many people thought at first that free libraries were a "frivolous entertainment", politicians supported the Free Libraries Act in 1882. Excitement surrounded the opening of the Toronto Public Library in 1884, but children under age fourteen were not allowed to enter.

black leather bag and then examined Lillian carefully. If she had been cut, the doctor might have plucked a horsehair from the animal's tail to sew stitches, but she was fine.

Lillian was more worried about the condition of her book than herself.

As she grew older, she carried with her into adulthood, this magnetic magic she felt towards children's books. Her passion for story never faltered in her desire to share these wonderful experiences. Her goal brightened with the years as she blended this focus with her mother's music and her father's religious zeal.

Bringing books and children together became the magical, musical mission of Lillian's life.

The Magical, Musical Mission

At first this mission seemed impossible. In the early 1900s, most people, including children, worked long hours just to have enough food, clothing and shelter. Welfare did not exist to help the struggling poor. Children could be seen on the streets selling newspapers or shining shoes. Many stopped school early to help their families.

Children's books were considered a waste of time. Even the new public libraries banned children under fourteen.

Girls especially, were not encouraged to be educated. They were raised to be wives and mothers, often finding work as a housekeeper before they reached high school. Only recently, just in time for Lillian, had women been allowed into the University of Toronto.

Being a bright and determined learner, she became one of the few women to graduate in 1910 from Victoria College at the University of Toronto. Still, she didn't know exactly what type of job she wanted. Then, flipping through a magazine, she saw an intriguing article.

"A course for Children's Librarians," the magazine announced. Lillian pulled the page closer. Reading further she discovered that the Carnegie Public Library in Pittsburgh, in the United States, had just opened a training school.

IMPOSSIBLE THINGS

The Queen: "Now I'll give you something to believe. I'm just one hundred and one years, five months and a day old."

"I can't believe that!" said Alice.

"Can't you?" the Queen said in a pitying tone. "Try again: draw a long breath and shut your eyes."

Alice laughed. "It's no use trying," she said. "One can't believe impossible things."

"I daresay you haven't had much practice," said the Queen. "When I was your age, I always did it for half an hour a day. Why, sometimes, I've believed as many as six impossible things before breakfast."

-Lillian read these words in *Alice in Wonderland* by Lewis Carroll, illustrated by John Tenniel

FATHER

Lillian modelled herself after her father. Well versed in Bible stories, he also collected the best in literature. Ahead of his time, he never spanked his children but found a gentler persuasive way to discipline. An intelligent, respected man, he spoke from the pulpit with a magnetic voice and kind manner. Her father, unlike her mother, lived to see Lillian become a successful children's librarian in Toronto.

VOTE FOR THE FREE LIBRARY

Here was a job where she could use her education, work with children and promote books. She had found the perfect career, but would she be accepted? The school only took twenty-five students.

The important acceptance letter arrived, making Lillian the only Canadian in this new course.

The train, zooming at its top speed of fifty-four miles per hour, jostled her on the hard bench. Her book bag was heavy with her old friends, including the well-worn copy of *Household Stories*. Lillian instinctively believed that children's books could change the life of any child, rich or poor. She must have been looking forward to meeting people who shared her intense interest. She wasn't disappointed.

Hardly noticing the smoke stacks of the steel mills, the students talked and talked. Together they enjoyed the twists and turns of the Greek story *Ulysses*. Lillian thought this was one of the greatest adventures of all time. Later, they talked about fairy tales. Lillian remarked that, interestingly, there were no fairies in them.

Not unlike her father giving a sermon, Lillian spoke with commitment. Her soft, powerful voice captivated everyone. With her blue eyes shining, she preached, "Children and books need each other!" Her mission had begun.

Steam locomotive in Union Station, Toronto

New York, New York

Anne Carroll Moore as a young librarian in 1906

THE PERFECT GIFT

In 1920, the staff of the Central Children's room in New York gave Anne Carroll Moore a Christmas gift. The Dutch Boy, an 8" high wood puppet, wore blue pants, a tiny scarf, a helmet and a grey jacket stitched around the edge with red wool. Anne immediately adored him and called him Nicholas.

Anne Carroll Moore was a little older than Lillian, but her life had taken a similar path. She had watched youngsters sitting on the library window sills, peering into the new public places as though mesmerized by the strange ritual. Their parents selected books, presented their ticket and had the books stamped with purple ink. Then the adults came out carrying these stories, which they "owned" for a few weeks.

When Anne became a children's librarian, she set about welcoming these youngsters into the new children's rooms. In need of a helper, she wrote to the principal of Lillian's school. Lillian had the knowledge of library work, an understanding of children and the necessary self-confidence. She was the star graduating student. So, in September 1911, Lillian Smith travelled to the city near the Statue of Liberty.

Here in New York, she met the outgoing, charming, dedicated, sometimes eccentric, Anne. Immediately, their similar interests made these two women bond in a lasting friendship.

Storytelling

FAIRY GODMOTHER

Marie Shedlock was a famous storyteller in the early 1900s. Dressed in a frilly costume, she related the stories of Hans Christian Andersen. Known as the Fairy Godmother of Storytelling, she later wrote a famous book, *The Art of the Storyteller.*

UNQUESTIONABLY

"The story hour is unquestionably one of the best methods of attracting children to books."

-Lillian Smith

OPEN SESAME

Many popular phrases come from fairy tales: A Cinderella tale; He's an ugly duckling; The goose that laid the golden egg; Beauty and the beast; Open sesame.

One program especially impressed Lillian. Anne had revived the ancient custom of storytelling. Long before books were printed, people all over the world had gathered to hear stories. Around campfires, in huts and homes, history and culture have been captured in oral folklore. Then this art was lost in most communities. Anne and Lillian revived the art of oral storytelling. Lillian Smith, with her wonderful voice and a mind that memorized with ease, became a captivating storyteller.

Sitting in the circle, Lillian didn't use props or dramatics. Her voice and eyes painted the pictures. "*Ulysses realized that the lantern was a great flaming eye. Then he saw the whole giant, tall as a tree...*" she began, as a few boys at the back shuffled, "*...with huge fingers reaching out of the shadows, fingers bigger than baling hooks.*" The boys giggled. Ignoring their antics, Lillian lowered her voice and directed her words to them.

"*They closed around two sailors and hauled them screaming into the air. As Ulysses and his horrified men watched, the great hand bore the struggling men to the giant's mouth.*" All the children sat spellbound. Even the trouble-makers at the back froze, mesmerized as they waited for more.

Afterwards, the children gathered around her, wanting to tell which part they liked best. Lillian encouraged them to explore why they favoured one scene. Books like *Ulysses* flew off the shelves. The line-ups for storytime grew and grew. Even in winter, children braved the bitter cold to hear Lillian tell a tale. Many had never before heard a story told out loud.

After only three weeks of training, Anne trusted Lillian to oversee the Children's Room in the Washington Heights Branch. Both children and adults noticed this new librarian's expertise. Her reputation spread from library to library and from the United States north to Canada.

THE DEWEY DECIMAL SYSTEM

Melvil Dewey, a librarian, thought that books, like people, should have addresses. Introduced in 1883, his system gave each book the same number in every library. You can always find fairy tales, for example, on the 398 shelf.

"Everyone wants it," one child said after Lillian read *Pinocchio*. Lillian wished she had dozens of these classic books on the shelves. She also wished the children could take home more than one fiction book, but Anne promoted non-fiction. Like most educators and librarians in the early 1900's, Anne wanted children to learn information. Teachers and librarians did not encourage the reading of Lillian's favourites, the type of story which sparked the imagination.

Children seemed to agree with Lillian. Books like *Robinson Crusoe* and *Gulliver's Travels*, originally written for adults, quickly captured young hearts. These were the tales Lillian promoted, the ones filled with adventure and imagery. She didn't think non-fiction was more important to a child than a fairy tale.

Still, the popularity of these books intrigued Lillian. Why, she wondered did immigrant children, whether Irish, Jewish or Italian, like *Pinocchio, Ulysses, Household Stories* and *Gulliver's Travels* just as much as she had as a child? Why did some stories cross generations and cultural tastes? Why did some books have everlasting life?

Oh, Canada

While Lillian pondered the popularity of the classics, another innovative thinker was making changes in Canada. Dr. George Locke, as the new Chief Librarian of the Toronto Library Board, had introduced open shelves and lowered the age for welcoming children. He had heard about the Children's Rooms in New York and about a talented young Canadian named Lillian Smith. He sent her a letter. Would Lillian come to Toronto and help him set up Children's Rooms in Toronto? Lillian's "yes" came quickly.

Anne Carroll Moore was disappointed to return from a trip to discover that she would lose Lillian as a librarian. She knew they would always remain friends. Anne organized a farewell picnic on Coney Island. The same children who had disturbed Lillian's first storytelling joined them for an afternoon of fun and stories and a sad good-bye. Anne gave a farewell speech which ended with these words: "Lillian, admit to no discouragement!"

Lillian could still hear these words echoing in her mind, as the train chugged its way north. She would need words of wisdom now that changes were unfolding all around her. Her mother had just passed away. Her father was living in Montreal. In Toronto, she would be on her own, but having this strong goal gave her strength and determination.

The train rocked, lulling her to sleep. As her eyes closed, she thought again about the classic books. What, she wondered, makes them so popular?

The First

THE EMPIRE

In Lillian Smith's time, one quarter of the world's population, Canada included, was a part of the British Empire.

In September 1912, at the age of twenty-five, Lillian H. Smith became the first children's librarian in the British Empire.

She walked up the broad staircase of the Carnegie-funded library and opened the huge double doors. Shining marble steps led to a vestibule that overlooked an enormous, bright room. Like a cathedral in its grandness, the high ceilings stretched three stories up to carvings, gilded with artistry. Light flooded through the windows lining an entire wall. She tread lightly in her high-laced boots, trying not to make an echo.

The smell of oak and old books reminded her of the library at home. Underneath the windows, shelves held books below and plants above. Long, banquet-type tables set in rows had extra lights at either end. Huge archways framed the back alcove. Andrew Carnegie's image and an old photo of Queen Victoria stared down from the wall.

A sense of hushed importance hung in the air. The silence announced that important things happened in this room.

The Toronto Reference Library, where Lillian began working in 1912

ANDREW CARNEGIE

A man who made a fortune in the steel industry, Andrew Carnegie donated millions to the building of libraries all over the world. He wanted not just to give charity but to wipe out the causes of ignorance. By 1919 he had built over 2,800 libraries in the U.S., Canada, Great Britain, Tasmania, New Zealand and the Fiji Islands. All over Canada, the early Carnegie Libraries sprouted, with their greystone fronts and columned entrances.

Some people said, "Children don't belong here." A few librarians didn't understand what Lillian would be doing. They had looked after the older children's questions just fine, they thought.

Lillian looked forward to welcoming children into this grand room and forged ahead with her plans.

Luckily, Dr. George Locke believed in the importance of children's books. He announced the good news to the papers. Headlines blared: "TORONTO LIBRARIES ARE TO CATER TO CHILDREN'S WANTS."

Not only tall in height, Dr. Locke's outgoing personality and expansive spirit equalled Lillian's. His topcoat, always open to the wind, made black wings of his jacket as he breezed into the large room. He wore a hat and swung his walking cane up and out and down in rhythm.

Greeting Lillian, he told her about new rules passed in 1909. Children could now use their own cards, known as tickets. Even younger children would be allowed into the library.

Lillian beamed one of her generous smiles. Then Dr. Locke continued to say that children's books were good for individuals and good for the country. One of these children might be the next Prime Minister. Children's books could affect the future of Canada and even the world. Lillian nodded total

DR. GEORGE LOCKE

Dr. George Locke introduced many changes. He recommended open shelves, allowing people to handle the books. Many on the Library Board said the old indicator system, with its book list, was working fine. People used to request a book choice from a list, and the librarian brought it to them. They said open shelves would be unsanitary. They worried about books being stolen. Dr. Locke persisted and set up the first open shelves in a Toronto Public Library.

agreement. Dr. Locke left her in charge of her department.

Then she realized that there was no glamour or promise in the messy book piles called the children's collection. Before her were tattered and torn copies, donated gifts or publishers' remainders, books they could not sell. Even the children's "room" was really just a dark alcove. Lillian controlled two other collections in local libraries, but they too were disappointing. No one before her had cared which books children read.

"Admit to no discouragement," she remembered Anne saying. For Lillian, obstacles only heightened her sense of challenge. The children's rooms opened at 9 a.m., and she worked long after the 6 p.m. closing time. Luckily, Toronto's night streets had just been brightened with new electric lights.

The word "literature" rolled off her tongue as she purchased the classics. *Gulliver's Travels* and *Household Stories* headed the list, and as many copies of *Pinocchio* as the budget allowed. Lillian felt children's books should entertain and delight while engaging the imagination.

Then, just as if she had played a Pied Piper tune, the children came in droves.

AN INDIVIDUAL

"The Children's Room is about the only place where a child comes as an individual, with tastes and interests. Is it not the library's responsibility to provide the books that will give his imagination, intelligence, curiosity and experience satisfactory material to grow on?"

-Lillian Smith

Older siblings holding the hands of younger children thronged into the small space. At lunch time, often a hundred children packed into the alcove. Lillian Smith made a point of leaving her desk if there was a child in need of help. She whispered, "Have you read this book?" Lillian found a good book for every child.

Gradually, she was answering her own questions, "Why are some books favourites forever? How do you choose a good children's book?"

A busy Saturday morning in the Riverdale Public Library in Toronto

Call Me Miss Smith

A PROMISE

"I resolved never to appear busy, while there was a child in the room."
-Lillian Smith

"Miss Smith, how do thermos bottles keep things hot?"

"Miss Smith, why do we lose a day between Vancouver and China?"

"Why do rabbits change colour in winter?"

"Do you have another book like *Alice in Wonderland?*"

The children's eyes radiated respect as she helped them find the answers.

Soon parents and other adults were asking questions: "Miss Smith, which book would make the best birthday present?"

Dr. George Locke, as well as her first three assistants and many visitors, approached this woman of knowledge. "Miss Smith, could you recommend a book for my daughter?" Soon her friends, neighbours and acquaintances were calling her Miss Smith.

The name stuck. Even the two librarians she would eventually live with, Margaret Johnston and Jean Thomson, called her Miss Smith. For the rest of her life, Lillian became Miss Smith.

The Forest of Firsts

CHEATED

"How can we make sure that no child is cheated of his inheritance of fine books?"

-Lillian Smith

Over the next forty years, Miss Smith took this small space in the corner of the main Toronto library at St. George and College Street and developed it into a world-renowned centre.

Like a gardener, she planted a forest of new ideas. Many of her ideas we now take for granted. Many of her thoughts are considered common sense. You probably walk in this established forest daily. You probably are enjoying its fruits, finding comfort in its shade, viewing beauty in its language and collecting knowledge in its leaves.

Every time you find a children's section in the library, every time you see stocked shelves, every time you are delighted by a puppet show, you are entering Lillian Smith's "forest".

Come, see how this "forest" grew to be a natural part of our lives.

Crowding soon became a problem at the St. George Street reference library.

Lillian Smith's Forest of Firsts

The Library Tree: For Children Only
The People Tree: The Best of the Best
The Book Tree: The Classics and More
The Learning Tree: Forever Changing
The Spreading Tree: Around the World
The History Tree: Past, Present and Future

Number One

The Library Tree:
For Children Only

CHILDHOOD

"Childhood is the formative period—the time when children are taking in impressions which affect their tastes, their standards and their outlook on life. Can we afford to be indifferent to the impressions they are gaining from the books they read?"

-Lillian Smith

As soon as Roger saw Miss Smith, he opened his palm wide. Five pennies shimmered. He had just enough money for a library card. The boy took off his cap and followed Miss Smith into the grand entrance. Roger felt a twinge of fear, because the grand room reminded him of a train station, and he felt he was on a journey.

At the desk, Roger told Miss Smith that the pennies had taken him over a month to save. Miss Smith completed his application and told him that his card would arrive by mail.

Roger watched daily as the postman pushed the envelopes through the slat in his front door. "It hasn't come yet, and I want to take out *Pinocchio*," he told Lillian.

Finally he came in waving his special card. He was officially a member of the library.

"We have to debate the fact that 'Wealth is better than knowledge.' The girls are arguing against." Roger kept talking as he made room for a friend on the long bench. "Before the last debate, the girls came to the library every day and then, when the debate took place,

CHILD LABOUR

The idea that children must have time to learn and enjoy entertainment was new for many struggling families. In the early 1900s, children often worked outside the home.

BIG GAP

In Toronto, some wealthy people enjoyed a post-Victorian upper class lifestyle. At the same time, a survey of houses in Toronto taken in 1934 found that

    59% had no bath
    20% had outside toilets
    55% had vermin
    82% had no central heating
    75% of the dwellings fell below proper health standards

they beat us all to pieces. This time we want to win."

Then just as this group was settled with the right books, a new little person stood shyly at Miss Smith's desk, "How much does it cost to take out a book?"

As Lillian developed the children's library, the children themselves learned how to use this unique place. One day Roger whispered to Lillian, "This library is home to me."

Children poured into the library at lunch, after school and on Saturdays. Smaller and smaller children scrambled up the broad staircase. Some of them flipped through the picture books. Older children came to do research, study or take out one of Miss Smith's "good" books.

Dr. George Locke proudly brought visitors to see this popular place and the capable young librarian. They arrived, most of them from a British background, in fashionable suits and bowler hats. One visitor, steeped in the British class system, found the poor children in the library difficult to accept. A few children weren't dressed neatly and appeared to be dirty, even smelly. Many of the homes in Toronto didn't have proper heating or plumbing.

Rich or poor, new immigrant or great-grandchild of a duke, Miss Smith welcomed them all. Every child, she believed, deserved a good book.

The War

"War!" Posters announced on August 4, 1914. Horses, wagons and a few black cars moved aside for marching crowds. Miss Smith could hear people singing "Britannia Rules the Waves" and "God Save the King." Caught up in the wave of nationalism and heroism, Roger's father, along with many Canadians, signed up to fight.

Since his father had worked for Eaton's, Roger's family received his father's full wage. Luckily, this meant Roger was able to continue his library visits, although his reading interests had changed. "How does a submarine work? Can we make a periscope? What is the new aircraft called? How does a bomb work?" Miss Smith was quick to order books about bombs and tanks, airplanes and submarines.

"Where is Ypres?" Roger asked. Miss Smith pulled down a rolled map like a window blind.

"What can we do to help?" Roger asked one day. Miss Smith showed the children how to start their own garden. Roger had never grown anything. Even a potato plant with its little sprouts excited him. Progress reports of these gardens lined the walls.

World War I submarine

FUTURE CITIZENS

"Whoever serves children in any capacity...is haunted by an awareness of a commitment to the future. Dealing with adults one works with the here and now. Each child wraps about him the promise or the threat of all that is yet to happen."
-Lillian Smith

Roger's name zoomed to the top of the charts. At story hour he talked about plants, telling how large they were, how thankful his mother was for the food. Growing a war garden made life at home easier.

Story hour now included patriotic tales. The adventures of the early explorers and Canada's heroes became popular. Miss Smith felt these stories helped children to be "intelligent citizens." After each tale, Miss Smith encouraged the children to donate non-perishable food so that they could prepare packages to send overseas.

So the children made it through the war from 1914-1918 feeling safe, while waiting for their fathers. They listened to stories, grew gardens, prepared donations and most of all, read and read.

After the War

CLIMB THE LADDER

Each child received a paper ladder with his or her name. When they finished a book, they got a green star for the next rung. A gold star went to those who had read five books and completed their ladder. Those with gold stars made the honour roll, a list pinned up in a special spot.

One day as Roger was coming home from the library, he saw Tommy Church going up his front steps. Why would the mayor be visiting his family? The news was not good. His father would not be coming back. Over nine million men died in this war which was supposed to end all wars.

Roger's father was one of the many fathers, brothers and future husbands who remained overseas, to sleep forever in Flanders Fields. Futures changed. Most of the young women working in the library had hoped to marry and have a family. Since married women didn't work outside the home, they knew they would have to leave the library. Now, with few men of marrying age left, young women outnumbered the men. Lillian Smith and a trusted group of friends, without mates, became lifetime, dedicated librarians.

Tommy Church, Mayor of Toronto, in the middle with the hat, says goodbye to a group of soldiers during the war.

Shakespeare

Roger spent more time at the library. One day he asked: "Say, wasn't Shakespeare an Englishman? I said he was and Jerry here said he wasn't."

"Well, I didn't know Shakespeare was English. I thought he was an Irishman...but even then he would have been a Britisher, just the same." Jerry said.

When Roger and Jerry returned, there was a display about Shakespeare. The boys discovered that Shakespeare was born in 1564 in Stratford-upon-Avon, England. They flipped through his biographies and the history of his times and his complete works, with illustrations. Jerry giggled at his collar. Then they viewed a picture of the open air stage. Miss Smith told them that Shakespeare was the greatest writer of all time. She introduced them to Charles Lamb's version, Shakespeare's stories written for children. Then she read from *The Tempest* and *Hamlet* at story hour. Much later she arranged performances of these plays in Little Theatre.

Displays, Miss Smith realized, were another way to connect books and children. She continued to set up tables of theme-related material to introduce a topic or author.

William Shakespeare

BOOKS ARE FUN

Shakespeare said, "How shall we beguile the lazy time, if not with some delight?" Lillian Smith agreed that children's books weren't just information packages. She helped children seek joy in stories.

DAY BOOKS

Miss Smith gave her librarians a black bound book. Each page had a red margin line and blue writing lines. These day books listed the number of books children borrowed and the happenings of the day. Personal stories of the children seeped into many reports. "Snub the cat is a favourite with the children and purrs during story time... Some of the children bring flowers to the library... Many of the children considered it a high honour to straighten the shelves. They have their own ideas of order..."

Christmas transformed the library. Piano concerts and singalongs were a part of the festivities. Red and green decorations filled the children's section. Then Miss Smith laid out a display of good children's books, which she recommended as holiday gifts. The Christmas Book Display became an annual event. People didn't buy gifts until Miss Smith laid out her sample holiday booklist.

And so the Library Tree, like a real tree in a forest, grew large and strong, branching out in all directions. The children's rooms filled with fun and festivities, sprouting displays, book clubs, storytelling and readings. Then it all came to an abrupt end.

Influenza Pandemic

HEALTH

In the early 1900's, bathing and showering facilities were not readily available, and many people didn't wash regularly. Schools held daily hand inspection. The teacher marched down the aisles as the children held out their hands, palm up. Then they flipped their hands over. A few times a year, a school nurse arrived for further health tests.

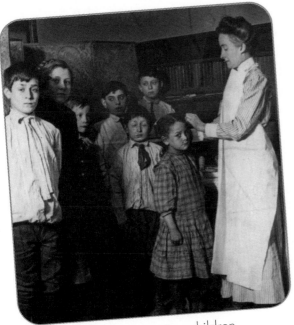

A nurse inspecting children at a Toronto public school

Roger didn't come to the library for a week. Jerry told Miss Smith that he had the flu. In 1918, "Spanish influenza" hit Canada hard. Returning troops brought this terrible germ over the ocean. More people died from this virus than from the First World War. Spreading quickly, it blanketed the world. At first, the sickness was called an epidemic; but it became so big, killing so many people, that the word pandemic was applied.

Luckily, Roger got better. Still, his mother would not allow him to return to the library. She was afraid. The flu had killed over thirty million people around the world. She didn't want Roger to go places where there were a lot of children. Research has proven that books are too dry to spread germs, but Roger's mother didn't know that. Other children were warned against going to the library. Miss Smith locked the doors.

Outside, children skipped rope and sang:

> I had a little bird,
> Its name was Enza.
> I opened the window,
> And in-flu-enza.

For Miss Smith the song echoed sadly off the neat, untouched shelves.

For Children Only

CHECK OUT

Each book had a pocket glued in the back. There was a slip in this pocket, pink for fiction and blue for non-fiction. The children used the little pencils provided on tables near the check-out desk to sign their names. The librarian stamped the due date on the slip, removed it for their record and then stamped the pocket in the book.

LIBRARY GOOP

From a newspaper article of Oct. 20, 1917:

"The little ones are taught not to be 'library goops'. That is, they must have clean hands, not snatch books off the shelves, be quiet and well behaved and not chew gum."

Finally, the pandemic scare came to an end. Miss Smith and the children returned to the alcove. For ten years she worked in this corner space as the demand for children's books grew. Line-ups for story hour stretched down the steps and around the block.

Now that Roger was older, he used the new reference area in the hallway. He had to run to the library after school to make sure to get a chair.

Children were turned away if the library was full. If only Miss Smith could have a separate large library just for children. Then she'd have a room for storytelling, a place for research, reading tables and picture collections. She could invite entire classes to this new library. There would be more displays, as well as a place to show art, make puppets and present plays. There would be room for a resource centre for parents and teachers.

As she imagined all these possibilities, the space situation became desperate. By 1920, the library was turning children away.

Miss Smith approached challenges as gentle battles to be won with words. Together she

BOOKPLATES

Bookplates are decorative labels with the owner's name. From the 1700s well into the 1900s, these popular art forms were pasted onto the front flap of books.

and Dr. Locke told the board about a separate library just for children. Unfortunately, the money donated by Andrew Carnegie, which had helped build so many libraries in Canada, was not available after 1917.

The members asked, "Does any other city have such a library? Why should we spend all that tax money? Is it that important?"

Then, a new law called the Public Libraries Act made more funds available. By then the board members had heard Lillian's soft yet powerful voice explain the benefits of such a library. They voted.

Toronto would have the first exclusive library for boys and girls in the entire British Empire.

LILLIAN SMITH'S OWN CLASSIFICATION

Miss Smith invented her own system of "addresses" for children's books. Adopted in 1931, her system made it easy for children to find their choices. Even a very young child knew the big X marked the spot for picture books.

By 1970, all books needed to be under the same system. The original conversion to the LHS method took a few months, but the change back to the Dewey Decimal System lasted years.

Lillian Smith's Classification System:

X   Picture Books
Z   Little Children's Books
A   Fairy Tales
C   Myths
D   Epic Heroes
F   Biography
G   History
H   Geography and Travel
K   Natural History
L   Science
N   Practical Science
O   Things to Do
P   Art
Q   Music
R   Plays
S   Poetry
W   Standard Works
     Fiction

Building a Dream

Roger held up the headline of *The Toronto Daily Star*: CHILDREN'S LIBRARY, THE FIRST IN CANADA, IS SHORTLY TO BE ESTABLISHED IN TORONTO.

Renovations to an old Victorian House at 40 St. George Street were completed on September 11, 1922. *The Evening Telegram* said, FOR CHILDREN ONLY.

Everyone talked about this strange new place. "It's called Boys and Girls House." In her office on the second floor, Miss Smith began to organize this huge dream into an efficient reality.

There was a special room with a fireplace just for story hour. She ordered lower shelves and smaller furniture, always thinking about the comfort of each child. Canadian art lined the walls. Reading circles, especially for the older group, expanded into Shakespeare studies and debating clubs. A separate space for reference material attracted children doing research. Parents and educators explored a section designed for them.

"Can I come too?" Roger asked Miss Smith as he dropped off his sister Janet.

"Sorry, Roger," she said. "You now belong in the adult section."

ROLE MODELS

"Give to the untrained mind of a girl
a heroine who is a sentimental,
tearful, wholly dependent maid, or to
the boy, stories of adventure in which
the heroes in the spirit of bravado
perform daring, foolhardy deeds, and
you will create false ideas and
destroy the very purpose of a
children's department."

-Miss Jessie Potter, speaking
to librarians in 1911.

"Do not make a sharp distinction
between books for boys and books
for girls, remembering that the books
that live are universal."

-Lillian Smith

Since there were no Young Adult books at
that time, Roger moved directly into the main
library. Roger had felt proud the first time a
librarian had taken his hand and directed him
to the adult section, saying, "You are ready for
some of these books."

Now when he saw all the new offerings for
children, Roger said, "I wish I'd had a Boys
and Girls House."

Follow the Leader

NOT A RIPPLE

"Not a ripple that affected children's reading escaped Lillian Smith's eagle eye and sensitive heart."
-Sheila Egoff

For Boys and Girls House to develop smoothly, Miss Smith attended to details, large and small. She knew how to deal with books, how to persuade people and how to keep order in the library. Her charisma, her enthusiasm, her motherly encouragement and demands pulled others to her cause. She was more than an administrator or manager; she became a good friend. She was not just a talker; she listened. She was not just a lover of books; Lillian Smith was a leader. Under her leadership, this Library Tree rooted deeply into our society, into the Forest of Firsts.

"I'm glad I have Boys and Girls House," said Janet. Then she whispered, "Can Roger stay some time?"

FUN AT BOYS AND GIRLS HOUSE

In the early 1900s, children had few organized programs for their free time. Except for the odd radio show, children entertained themselves with sports, games, puzzles and imaginary adventures. Going to the library was fun. They eagerly lined up in front of Boys and Girls House.

THE GREAT DEPRESSION

The Great Depression began in 1929 when the stock market crashed. In Toronto, one out of every four people, was unemployed. Line-ups at charity soup kitchens grew. People flocked to the library. Not only were they looking for shelter, but they also hoped to find information about work.

The interior of a poor Canadian home during the depression

PROBLEMS

In the 1930s, the purchasing of new books and expansion of the library system stopped. For Miss Smith, space and money always remained the two major problems.

Number Two
The People Tree:
The Best of the Best

Betty, a teenager, prepared for a job interview with Miss Smith. She put on her finest white blouse, buttoned and ruffed to the neck, and her long grey skirt. She wished she didn't have to leave school, but her father was ill, and it was the 1930s. These years, known as The Great Depression, left thousands jobless and penniless. What would Miss Smith ask her, she wondered.

With her mother by her side, Betty boarded the red streetcar. She peered out the window. Families lived in cardboard shelters on the streets. Weary, bedraggled people formed long lines waiting for free soup. Betty's whole family depended on her getting a job. She hoped she'd have the answers to Miss Smith's questions.

Boys and Girls House looked like a pleasant place to work. Children returned books in the porch area. Betty could see that children, their needs and their interests came first. The shelves looked tidy and organized under Miss Smith's own special classification system. Betty wanted to pause at the table with books about Marco Polo, but she was directed upstairs to Miss Smith's office.

She and her mother waited in the outer room. Then the secretary told Betty to enter.

From the far corner, a growl made her jump. Tommy, Miss Smith's curly-haired black spaniel, reared his head. Betty tried not to show her surprise at seeing a dog in the office. Miss Smith stood upright and fiddled with her glasses. Betty felt fear creep up her spine.

Then Miss Smith spoke. Her voice was relaxing, soft and gentle. "Why did you apply for this job? What school subjects do you like?

FIVE DAY WEEK

Librarians worked all day and then, without extra pay, ran a school club or spoke to a group in the evening. The shortened five day week did not start for them until 1950.

What is your favourite children's book? Do you read a lot? What are your interests? Would you prefer to persuade or discipline children?"

Miss Smith's searching blue eyes remained fixed on Betty.

"Persuade," Betty said, answering the last question.

Miss Smith's face lit up with a full, fascinating smile. "Take a tour of Boys and Girls House." As Betty walked through all the rooms, she realized that the lending library, the reading room, the reference area and the story room were all designed for a child's comforts, all tailored to topics children enjoyed.

When Betty returned to the office, she found her mother and Miss Smith sharing the English tea time tradition. "If you pass your exams in June," Miss Smith laid down her cup, "you can come and work here in September. You will be paid $12.00 a week."

All the way home, Betty felt saddened by the scene of depression around her, but she felt glad that her family was safe for now.

Would she be able to learn the duties? Could she keep up with the reading material? Most of all, she was anxious about storytelling. Getting up in front of a group to speak filled her with shyness.

Miss Smith had set up a program by which trainees learned from a senior staff member. So learning the library routine was easier than Betty had thought. Betty read voraciously. Still, she worried about storytelling. She feared she just wouldn't be able to do it.

She didn't have too much time to worry because a little girl was tugging at her skirt.

"Teacher, find me, an awful, terrible scary book about witches and things." Betty was already used to being called teacher, and she knew which book to recommend. She pulled down the well-worn copy of *Household Stories.*

A Tour of Boys and Girls House

Boys and Girls House

The children entered through the sun porch where they returned books. The two front rooms held the circulating collection.

Behind these were the reading and reference rooms. As well as reference books, there were special editions of illustrated books. The Fairy Tale Room was for the younger children. It had picture books, fairy tales and simple stories. Spread over the long oak table was a map of Fairyland.

From the Fairy Tale Room, there was an entrance to Little Theatre. This was the place for story hour, staff meetings, puppet and shadow plays, play groups and interest clubs. Little Theatre, the new room at the back, held a model collection of children's books, a sample for visitors to study and copy. There was a fireplace at one end and the stage at the other. The mural on the wall, a jungle scene of animals, displayed the talents of the students from the Ontario College of Art.

The Second Floor held Miss Smith's office and all the administration offices. The third floor was a professional study area. Here librarians or researchers found appropriate material such as book reviews and articles.

Monday, Monday

JOYOUS

Miss Smith believed that "children's literature is not a pedantic or an academic study. It is a joyous, fruitful and endlessly rewarding field."

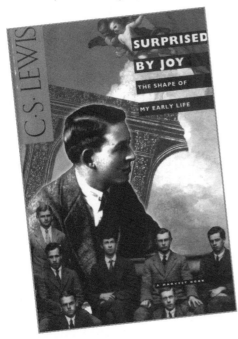

I LIKE IT

"If we limit children to our own tastes in reading, we pauperize their minds."

-Lillian Smith

Monday mornings, the entire staff gathered for their weekly meeting. With arms folded, Betty sat in the last row of the Little Theatre. Miss Smith stood at the front in her business-like blue suit. Once she spoke, all were drawn to her inspirational voice that contrasted with her plain appearance. She recommended that they read C.S. Lewis' book *Surprised by Joy*, to help them recall the joy of being a child. She wanted the librarians to relive the feeling of discovering a wonderful book. She reminded them that sharing great literature was a vital calling. They could redirect lives. Childhood was so short; their mission crucial. Betty settled into her seat and let her arms relax. A wave of enthusiasm swept over her. What an important job she had, after all!

Then a senior librarian introduced a book, a retelling of the *Three Billy Goats Gruff*. She explained that this tale was told without metaphors, sparse like the land of the Norse culture, where it originated. A lively debate about what makes a good retelling followed.

Betty watched closely. Each senior librarian had become an expert in one genre. One knew fantasies well, another was a science expert and yet another promoted the Greek legends.

Librarians hold a meeting in the storytelling room at Boys and Girls House

THE FIRST CANADIAN CHILDREN'S BOOK

Catherine Parr Traill wrote *Canadian Crusoes* in 1852. Printed in England, the book tells the story of children lost in the forest for three years.

What area would Betty choose?

After the debate, the librarians voted on whether to purchase the retelling. Then there were library issues to discuss. Was non-fiction more valuable than fiction? What about books in series? Was there a unique Canadian literature? While the group expressed opinions, Betty took a long look around the room. She understood why the children loved sitting here for Story Hour. The mural on the wall had lions and tigers that roared in lifelike vitality. The fireplace in the far corner looked warm and inviting.

Just then, Betty heard Miss Smith's voice overrule the others. Miss Smith was adding her final opinion. She said they should promote Canadian authors. The realistic animal stories, the folklore and the northern settings were unique.

Betty was sorry when the meeting was over. She enjoyed being a part of this group, just listening in the audience. Oh, but how she feared having to be the speaker. How long could she put off storytelling and book reviewing?

EARLY CANADIAN BOOKS

Titles of some of Canada's early children's books:

—*How the Carter Boys Lifted the Mortgage* (1894)

—*How Rank Did it, That Worthless Lad* (1898)

—*The Watchers of the Campfire* (1904)

—*The Backwoodsmen* (1909)

—*Jim, the Story of a Backwoods' Police Dog* (1919)

Most early books about Canada written for children were published in England or the United States and were animal stories, tales about the north and other regions of Canada, or about children having adventures.

Although public speaking scared her, Betty relished all the reading. She carried a book with her on the streetcar. She read at lunch in the park. She read at tea time in the map room. On her days off she read and read. Then, like the other librarians, she could pull down any book and tell the tale. She especially liked the Hans Christian Anderson fairy tales. She never tired of encouraging children to read "The Ugly Ducking" and "The Shoemaker and the Elves". One day she told the story "The Red Shoes" to a child.

"She danced and danced and was obliged to go on dancing through the dark night until she was all torn and bleeding" was its tragic ending. Both she and the child were so entranced that Betty didn't feel nervous. She had surprised herself. She was a storyteller after all.

"Now bend your neck and say 'Quack!'" An illustration from "The Ugly Duckling" by Hans Christian Andersen, 1899, illustrated by Helen Stratton

Goodbye, Tommy

SOMETHING NEW

In the 1930s, new school programs gave children the freedom to do research projects. Hordes of children swarmed the library, hunting for information on Marco Polo, the Huns and the Crusades.

Meanwhile Betty handled duties galore. She shelved the books in their correct spot. She learned Miss Smith's own classification system. A senior librarian checked her work and pulled out any misplaced books. Betty re-shelved them. She directed the children to the proper research material. She introduced them to the classic tales. Then she stamped the due dates onto the backs of books and reminded them about the late fine.

If she were asked to take Tommy for a walk, she hoped another librarian would come along. Tommy could be a good dog, but sometimes he liked to nip heels or growl at strangers. Betty feared he'd run off.

One day she was on her own with Tommy. The dog marched her around the block and stopped at a public water fountain. At this special fountain, the dog, Betty and a horse all drank at the same time. Betty held on tight to the leash but the dog drank calmly and then trotted back to the library.

A public water fountain on Spadina Avenue in Toronto

TEA AND TOMMY

Tommy was a black, curly-haired spaniel. He often huddled at Miss Smith's feet as she held meetings or shared the British afternoon tea tradition.

As they walked through the front door, Betty sighed with relief. They had made it back safely. Then, just as she let Tommy off the leash, he charged at a visitor. Betty gasped. Tommy ran after the man, nipping at his heels and tearing his pants.

This visitor happened to be Dr. Sanderson, the new chief librarian. Tommy was never allowed back into the library.

Stories, Plays, Puppets and Displays

THE CNE

In 1921, the Canadian National Exhibition invited Miss Smith and her staff to set up a storytelling tent. People from all over the country visited the CNE and the tent. Many returned home and organized story hours.

While Betty did her daily duties, she kept worrying about storytelling. She knew it would please Miss Smith to hear her tell a tale. Everyone looked forward to Miss Smith's smile of approval, and Betty was no exception. With her heart fluttering, she started to memorize "The Red Shoes". Miss Smith demanded the librarians know the story by heart. She rehearsed before the next staff meeting. At the Monday morning meeting, Betty's mouth felt as though it were glued shut. There were so many words to remember. What if her mind went blank?

She swallowed hard and took a deep breath. "*Once upon a time there was a little girl named Karen, pretty and dainty.*" Her voice grew louder and stronger. "*Come out, come out! I cannot come in, for I must dance.*" The last lines flowed. Betty finished without one mistake. All the librarians sat silently and stared at her. Then they clapped in unison. The whole room seemed to fill

"She could not stop herself." An illustration from Hans Christian Andersen's story "The Red Shoes"

48

STORYTELLING

Although most storytellers rely on images, changing the words slightly with each story repetition, Lillian Smith taught her librarians to memorize the words.

with joy. A proud sense of accomplishment washed over Betty. Miss Smith stood up. Her full smile showered Betty with approval and, in front of everyone, she invited Betty to tell the tale to the children on Saturday.

Saturday story hour was held in the Little Theatre. Betty sat near the fireplace with the children in a semi-circle around her. *"Don't cut off my head!' said Karen... 'I have suffered enough for the red shoes.'"* The sea of eyes before her grew wide and intent.

Things went so well that Miss Smith asked Betty to take the tale "on tour" to the other libraries. Again and again, Betty held a rapt audience like a magnet. Then she progressed to telling the older children ongoing stories, longer tales done in segments.

Confident now, Betty joined the theatre group. The stage in Little Theatre was fast becoming as popular as story hour. The children joined clubs, made sets, put on costumes and learned lines. It was here that some children started theatrical careers.

Special People

TRUST

Such an element of trust existed in the Toronto Public Library that one librarian worked for 46 years without a contract.

NO PICTURES PLEASE

One school visitor asked for a picture of the library. Miss Smith gave them a picture of her dog Tommy. She shied away from photos and shifted personal compliments to her staff.

SPECIAL LIBRARIANS

Mary Saxe, chief librarian at Westmount Library in Quebec, spent ten years persuading the committee to build a Children's Room. In her annual report in 1911 she wrote, "the greatest event in the library's history was the opening of the Children's Room."

LOVE

"The love for a good story, well told, lies deep in every human heart."
  -Lillian Smith

Betty never discovered the real reason Miss Smith had hired her during the first interview. Her apt answers to Miss Smith's questions helped her get the job, but there was more. Miss Smith knew this library needed special personalities. She looked for dedicated people who enjoyed children, lovers of literature who could inspire enthusiasm as well as promote books.

Miss Smith had this rare ability to predict a person's potential and pinpoint strengths. Then she knew how to encourage and develop these skills. "Lillian Smith made us feel important." The librarians felt they became better people and accomplished workers.

Although Miss Smith was the initiator and power behind every library undertaking, she stayed in the background. She rarely talked about herself, her feelings or her family. Praise, when it came her way, was always shared with her staff. When an important visitor, like a European princess, honoured Boys and Girls House, the librarians were included in the gatherings.

Betty and all the other librarians thrived under Miss Smith's guidance. They became knowledgeable and flexible, accommodating and stimulating—the best of the best children's librarians.

The Book Tree:
The Classics and More

RAREST KIND OF BEST

"Only the rarest kind of best in anything can be good enough for the young."

-Walter de La Mare

CHOOSING

"Children's books do not exist in a vacuum, unrelated to literature as a whole. They are a portion of universal literature and must be subjected to the same standards of criticism as any other form of literature. This is a literature of value and significance."

-Lillian Smith

What makes a book a good book for children? Miss Smith continued to ponder this question. The answer, she knew, must lie hidden in the forever-popular stories, the classics. These strong stories had stood the test of time.

She set up meetings to study these time-tested tales. She and her librarians discussed every aspect of these treasures. Is this book well-written? Why and how? What makes the character Long John Silver from *Treasure Island* scary? Does the story move along with action and intrigue? Is it exciting? Together, the group listed universal lasting literary qualities of these books.

The classics like *Treasure Island* remained Miss Smith's proven path to understanding good books. These books became the models. She called them the "Yardstick" books. New books were compared to these Yardstick books.

Betty was given *Dr. Dolittle* to review at the Monday morning staff meeting. Saying "I like this book," or "I don't like this book," was not good enough. Miss Smith demanded that each

A portrait of Long John Silver, the one-legged pirate, from *Treasure Island* by Robert Louis Stevenson, 1924, illustrated by Frank Godwin.

IS IT WORTHY?

"When a new children's book is heralded as another *Alice in Wonderland* or *Treasure Island* or *Tom Sawyer*,[its] claim to stand beside a well-loved favourite rests on the degree to which it possesses the magic of a Lewis Carroll or a Robert Stevenson or a Mark Twain."

-Lillian Smith

THE CLASSICS

"...those books which generations of children have taken to their hearts... books which seem to have an immortality."

-Lillian Smith

librarian explain why she liked or disliked a book.

As she'd been taught, Betty studied the plot, the use of beautiful language, character development and the structure of the book. She noted the musical and poetic quality of the words. Did the story draw word pictures in her mind? Did the story show place, culture or history? She measured its child appeal. Overall themes and messages became part of her presentation. Most importantly, how did this book compare to the great Yardstick books? She compared it to *Pinocchio* and *Treasure Island*. Were the characters as life-like? Was the story as interesting? Was the language as compelling?

Finally, Betty was ready to present her first book review. Betty now spoke to an audience with ease. She said that children would love this book about a doctor who spoke to animals. The idea would spark their imagination, bring them humour and delight. The characters were well-drawn and the story structure taut. She thought this selection lived up to the quality of the Yardstick books.

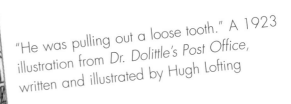

"He was pulling out a loose tooth." A 1923 illustration from *Dr. Dolittle's Post Office*, written and illustrated by Hugh Lofting

52

SOME YARDSTICK BOOKS

King Arthur Stories
Tom Sawyer
Treasure Island
Babar
Jonny Crow
The Railway Children
The Old Curiosity Shop
David Copperfield
Jane Eyre
Les Misérables
Tale of Two Cities
Shakespeare's Plays
Uncle Remus
The Wind in the Willows

ONLY THE BEST

"To tolerate the mediocre and the commonplace is to misunderstand the purpose of book selection..."
-Lillian Smith

The librarians had all read *Dr. Dolittle.* They debated, voted and approved Betty's book. *Dr. Dolittle* would be honoured with a place on the shelf of Boys and Girls House.

Each new book went through this long process. The title was studied, discussed, debated and most of all compared to the great books of all time. Only then could it take its place on the shelf beside the classics. No book was ordered from a catalogue, sight unseen, as long as Miss Smith lived and ruled.

Miss Smith said that a library which did not include the classics was in danger of promoting mediocre material. Boys and Girls House was no mediocre library; it was fast becoming the best library for children's books in the world.

A librarian sharing the classic tale *Madeline*

Books for Boys and Girls

WHO'S READING FICTION?

In 1933, children's book preferences went in this order:

Fiction
Nature books
History
Poetry
Heroic Tales

DID GIRLS READ THE SAME BOOKS AS BOYS?

In 1934, the Toronto Public Library conducted a study in which they learned that generally girls read more than boys and that boys read more non-fiction books than fiction. With the exception of a few titles, boys and girls read the same books of fiction and enjoyed the same stories at story hours.

Once her method of selection was operating smoothly, Miss Smith recorded a list of tested good books. This list itself became a book. *Books for Boys and Girls* was first published in 1927.

This text became required reading for librarians and educators. Parents liked it too. People working with children desperately needed such a guidebook. Some came to the library and went to the third floor where Miss Smith kept adult books about children's literature. Others requested information by mail. Boys and Girls House became a trusted, reliable resource centre for children's literature. Requests for information and books poured in from across Canada. As Lillian Smith's reputation spread, letters and requests arrived from countries around the world.

Number Four

The Learning Tree:
Forever Changing

Miss Smith stomped downstairs and plunked three reviews on Betty's desk. "You are a good reviewer, but you can't just clobber people." Miss Smith always gave a compliment before being critical. She expected Betty to do the same when she reviewed books for the Toronto Public Library Newsletter. Without objecting, Betty rewrote the reviews.

Betty learned much from Miss Smith, even how to handle awkward situations. Just as she was finishing the new reviews, a local branch frustrated her with their refusal to provide information. Betty had tried, but they kept blocking her request. Betty knew that one call from Miss Smith and the branch would jump to open its files. Betty asked Miss Smith to "please call them."

Miss Smith refused. She told Betty to find a way to convince the branch that the request was justified. Betty was upset at first. What else could she say to the branch librarian? She turned her finger reluctantly through the

Lillian Smith wearing her favourite hat

LIVING COLLECTION

Miss Smith called her library a "living collection" which, like a living organism, evolved and changed.

MOTHERLY CONCERN

Along with professional guidance, Miss Smith doled out motherly concern to her librarians. She was sympathetic to any signs of illness, giving them time off. When the library was being painted, she allowed them to go home if they found the oil-based paint smelled too strong. When Betty moved into a smaller apartment, where no animals were allowed, Miss Smith offered to care for her pet.

circular black phone dial. "Hello," Betty's voice quivered. Calmly, she repeated reasons for needing the information. Miss Smith's method worked. Next time, Betty would handle this type of problem on her own.

When Betty was called into Miss Smith's office she never knew what to expect. "You know," Miss Smith said one time, "I've arranged for a group to come to my place once a week. I think you would enjoy learning how to listen to music with my musician friend."

Another time she said, "I've arranged a course in poster making with a young Canadian artist named Doris McCarthy. I think you might like to go."

There was no end to these discoveries. Sessions included English country dancing, play reading and productions. Once she announced to her librarians, "You know some of you would enjoy a course in eurhythmics."

"I had to look up the word 'eurhythmics' in the dictionary," said Betty, "to find out it meant movement to music."

All of the staff working at Boys and Girls House spent their time off reading and learning. They all agreed: "She didn't let you get into a rut."

English country dancing

The Teacher and the Child

IS IT POISONOUS?

One child brought a mushroom to the
library. The librarian peeled and
smelled it and assured the child it was
not poison. Then next day the child
arrived with another specimen. The
librarian quickly found books on
mushrooms.

Many of the librarians knew Miss Smith from their early studies at the University of Toronto. When Dr. George Locke first introduced librarian courses in 1913, Lillian Smith was one of the first teachers. Until her retirement in 1952, she continued to lecture. She said, "I visualize children's librarians returning as students year by year to learn more." She inspired her students to read, enjoy, think and discuss. All her students remembered the way her special voice mesmerized them at Christmas as she read from *The Wind in The Willows.*

Some of her students came to work at Boys and Girls House, where they knew they would have to keep learning. "What a person works at, it is his duty to study," said Miss Smith.

Miss Smith was everywhere when children's books were involved. She juggled staff meetings, library association meetings and teaching. Even with this busy schedule, she never lost touch with the children themselves.

NO TIME TO WASTE

"In the case of children whose youthful and formative years are so brief there is little time to waste. Why give a child less than...value."

-Lillian Smith

ARE FAIRIES REAL?

After reading *The Water-Babies*, one girl looked troubled, "I want to ask you something," she said to the librarian. "I want to know the truth about fairies. Mother would make fun." The librarian looked at the child, sat down and whispered, "I do believe in fairies. Do you?"

On her routine visits to branch libraries, she spoke to the children, listened to their interests and suggested books. Then she came back to Boys and Girls House with an armload of books for her own reading.

One day she saw a shy girl wandering aimlessly through the collection. Miss Smith approached her and then realized it was Janet, Roger's sister. Miss Smith pulled down a book from one of the higher shelves and opened it like a birthday present. All the librarians paused to watch. Watching Miss Smith interact with a child was like watching a professional athlete. No one captivated a child with the same magnetic force. Immediately Janet forgot about being shy. "She was always trying to teach you something about books," Janet said.

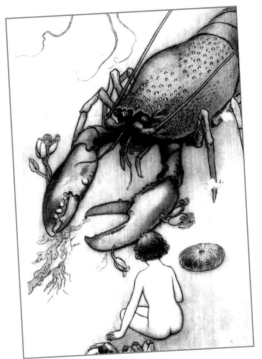

"Tom had never seen a lobster before."
A 1910 illustration from *The Water-Babies* by Charles Kingsley, illustrated by Warwick Goble

The Play's the Thing

PUPPETS AND MARIONETTES

Marionettes are wood puppets manipulated with strings. The children cut wood and sewed costumes in a messy but productive workshop. These elaborate puppets lined the library as displays. Then they came "alive" in library plays.

When Janet returned the book, she noticed dressed marionettes on the display tables. Some of them resembled the characters she'd just read about in *Peter Pan*. She longed to hold one of them, recreate the story and mouth the words she had just read. A librarian noticed her interest and invited Janet to attend puppet-making classes.

Little Theatre was transformed into a workshop. Banging and sawing brought Pinocchios to life. They learned how to carve, connect and string real marionettes. Janet dressed her puppet as Wendy from *Peter Pan* and prepared for the next performance. Janet couldn't handle all the strings herself, so one of the librarians helped. As Janet "played" the part, her shyness disappeared.

The "Three Little Kittens" and "Sleeping Beauty" became favourite plays for the younger club. The older group developed scenes from *Peter Pan*. Even the librarians joined in becoming actors at Christmas or at other celebrations.

The Shakespeare followers enjoyed producing *Julius Caesar* and *King Lear. The Tinder Box*, another popular play, was announced at two story hours and, on the performance day, 225 children were waiting in line.

FROM A SKIT FOR A LIBRARIAN'S FAREWELL PARTY

"She is the very model of a modern librarian
She's information animal, reptilian and aquarium
She knows the Kings of England and she quotes the fights historical
From Marathon to Waterloo in order categorical
She's very well acquainted too with matters mathematical
She understands equations both the simple and quadratical
For she is a librarian and it is a glorious thing to be."

Miss Smith's Little Theatre was the first opportunity these children had to connect with plays and the stage. Toronto's interest in young people's theatre had not yet developed. In the same way as Miss Smith was ahead of her time in valuing children's early reading and storytelling, she was also advanced in promoting role acting and plays. Here, those who stuttered forgot to pause in their speech. Here, the shy, like Janet, grew bold, and the talented spread wings. It wouldn't be until years later, in the 1950s, that children's plays like *Aladdin* found their way to the public stage at Eaton's Auditorium.

Teaching, learning, expansion and change touched everyone and everything in Miss Smith's path.

Number Five

The Spreading Tree: Around the world

HOUSES OF HELP

Settlement Houses sprouted to aid the growing numbers of immigrants. Before welfare existed, these newcomers depended on these places for guidance and aid. All types of programs, athletic, dramatic and educational, helped young and old adapt to their new country.

Strolling amongst the shelves, Miss Smith saw the Saturday morning group of children eagerly thumbing the books. Story hour was a continuing success, and she could see the large group embracing every word of *Beowulf*. Still, she was troubled. Hundreds of children came to the library, but there were hundreds who never made the trip. How, she wondered, could she get books to them?

At one table she saw a group of immigrant children huddled over picture books. The image reminded her of the government-run shelters. These Settlement Houses offered food and clothing, advice and programs to new Canadians. Why not have books in the Settlement Houses?

Once Miss Smith had an idea, it was only a matter of time before she made it a reality. Children's rooms in the Settlement Houses were

Storytime at Earlscourt Public Library in Toronto

ENRICHMENT

Miss Smith felt books were important because "...a child's active and ranging mind can find in books, and nowhere so well as in good books, the material to enrich the experiences of these years, in spite of the limited and uneventful environment which is the usual lot of childhood."

The title page of *Tales from Shakespeare*, by Charles and Mary Lamb.

soon decorated and stocked. While their parents learned English, the children delighted in learning their new language through stories and pictures.

By the 1930s, Miss Smith had opened libraries in all the Toronto Settlement Houses, such as St. Christopher's House and University Settlement. Later, after the Second World War, she took children's books to the new Canadians in the Hart House Reception Centre.

In these new libraries, children "read" the pictures and sorted out the ABCs of a new alphabet. Miss Smith invited these children to visit the big library. Many of these new immigrants had never been in a library. One young girl named Thelma arrived the very next day.

Thelma meandered around the tables, in awe of the number of book choices at Boys and Girls House. She read slowly, learning the language. Then she read avidly, devouring books by the dozens. Sometimes she loved a story so much she hated to give it back and renewed it over and over. How she longed for a book of her own.

She took her meagre weekly allowance and saved for months. She watched her friends go to the new series-type movies and listened to them talk about the next episode. She licked

THELMA'S OWN LIBRARY

The Old Curiosity Shop
David Copperfield
Jane Eyre
Les Misérables
Tale of Two Cities
Shakespeare's Plays
and many other books. On the inside
of each book, Thelma pasted her own
bookplate.

her lips as her friends ate lollipops. Finally she had saved enough to buy one book. Thelma continued to scrimp and save for more books.

When Thelma turned fourteen, Miss Smith honoured her by showcasing Thelma's library. This special display, entitled "A Girls Own Library", drew the attention of adults and children alike.

Thelma's book display gave Miss Smith much satisfaction. The Settlement Libraries were a success.

Still, she thought, there must be more children out there, somewhere, without books. Where and how could she find them? Miss Smith knew where to look.

A Girl's Own Library
(Courtesy of Thelma Gray)

Adventure
Folk Tales
Fantasy
Short Stories
for Boys and Girls

Into the Schools

With *Treasure Island* and an armload of books, Miss Smith walked into schools. She could imagine the questions forming in the young minds. Who was she? A new teacher? When Miss Smith spoke, her lovely voice caught their attention even before the rhythm of the words reached their ears. Just as the story peaked, she stopped. "What do you think will happen? How will the book end? Who would like to be the first to read this book?" Hands flew into the air.

For many of these children, this was their first book review. More than one child saw a path opening wide. This path led them into a forest of their imagination, into Miss Smith's Forest of Firsts.

After the school visit, she invited everyone to story hour at the library. She spoke to teachers about bringing the entire classroom to the library.

Schools all over the city requested these visits. Miss Smith delegated the job to her librarians. Children hovered around the librarians in the schoolyard. They caught glimpses of titles like *Beowulf, Canterbury Tales* and *Peacock Pie*. "Today we get storytelling," the children exclaimed.

Years later, Miss Smith had another idea.

Why not open small library branches right in the schools? The cost could be shared between the school and library boards.

Through her efforts, the first public library school branch opened in 1926 in Queen Victoria School in Toronto. A librarian went to the Parkdale area every Wednesday to unlock the tiny space. Only ten children fit in the room at one time, but they lined up patiently and waited their turn. Choosing a book for themselves was a new, exciting happening.

Even as these popular school libraries mushroomed, Miss Smith still wondered, "Where else are there children in need of books?"

Into the Hospitals

HUMOUR

Miss Smith promoted humour in children's books. Amongst her favourites were *Dr. Dolittle* and *Curious George,* which helped lift the spirits of hospitalized children.

In hospitals, Miss Smith found hundreds of children who couldn't come to Boys and Girls House. She heard about Leonard, a young boy with an injured spine. He had not been able to walk for three years. At first, Leonard refused to smile when Miss Smith visited the hospital. She took out *Aesop's Fables* and just read to him. Slowly he warmed to her weekly readings. "What a time they had with the books," said a nurse. Miss Smith now had another idea about reaching children.

In 1951, with 635 beds, the Hospital for Sick Children in Toronto was the largest children's hospital in North America. In her organized, caring manner Miss Smith trained librarians to enter the hospital, tell stories and suggest books. Two mobile book "trucks" carrying 250 books were wheeled from room to room.

Roger had grown up. His son Desmond, who had epilepsy, had to endure many tests at the hospital. One day Roger arrived to a smiling Desmond, who was reading *Curious George* to the child in the next bed.

"Where did you get that book?" Roger asked, "It used to be one of my favourites in the days of Miss Smith's library."

"The librarians come around with a book

The Hospital for Sick Children in Toronto

66

trolley," said Desmond. "I even got a book on epilepsy and medicine. Told me I'm smart and that I can lead a normal life."

Roger grinned. Even here, so many years later, Miss Smith was planting seeds of her great forest.

Desmond was lucky. With the proper medication, he returned to school. His roommate was not so lucky. Moved to the seventh floor isolation ward, he missed Desmond and the stories. The librarians and their book "trucks" were not allowed to enter these units.

"Admit to no discouragement," always remained Miss Smith's motto. She arranged for the old books, damaged or broken copies, to be put through a sterilization process. These were sent to the isolation wards, where they brought some glimmer of entertainment and hope.

The bookmobile was another way of bringing books to children everywhere.

Around the World

"One thing that puzzled us all," said one visitor, *"was how one small person, Lillian H. Smith, could have established such a powerful influence. [We] brought back her ideas, her standards, a firm belief in their importance and a copy of Books for Boys and Girls."*

Miss Smith's influence spread beyond Toronto. Educators and parents travelled from afar to use the information section on the third floor. Packages with library information made their way to remote areas of Canada.

Children's librarians from Britain, Japan, and Malaysia took part in an intern program which allowed them to study with Miss Smith for one year. Visitors from Australia, New Zealand and Tasmania came to the now famous house on St. George Street.

Mr. Leake, a wealthy man from Rhodesia in Africa, came to visit his daughter Mary, who was working at Boys and Girls House. He thought it would be wonderful to have such a library in Southern Rhodesia. He had the money; Miss Smith had the knowledge.

Miss Smith sent all her favourite books to Africa. This would be a test for her old friends Gulliver, Long John Silver, Alice and George. Would children raised in a totally different culture enjoy the classic tales? Just as Miss Smith had guessed, *Gulliver's Travels* and *Curious George* were just as popular in Africa as in Canada. She realized

The interior of Boys and Girls House

A good story has universal appeal.

BOMBED

Bethnal Green in East London, England, was bombed during the Second World War. Houses and schools were destroyed. The children had no books. Miss Smith raised funds and packed new books to send across the ocean.

once again that a good story has universal appeal.

At the end of one day, the African librarian found a boy in the corner engrossed in a book. "How long have you been here?"

"Since this morning," he answered. He begged the librarian to keep the book for him till tomorrow. "It's such a good book," he explained.

"Why don't you take it out?"

The boy didn't explain but asked again if she would keep it for him. The librarian nodded, wondering which title had kept him so engrossed. After the boy left, the librarian picked up the book and read the title, *The Adventures of Tom Sawyer*.

The Yardstick books remained favourites all over the world.

One visitor, Miss Momoko Ishii, a Japanese librarian, found herself absolutely intrigued by Boys and Girls House. In Japan, there were no special libraries for children. All Miss Smith's philosophies, ideas and programs impressed Miss Ishii. She envisioned herself as the Miss Smith of Japan. With armloads of information and books, she returned home to her remote village. High atop the mountain, she started sharing books with youngsters. To this day, Miss Smith's name is special in Japan. A Japanese video and several books honour her legacy.

Gifts

WHAT DO YOU CALL YOUNG PEOPLE?
From masters and misses
To boys and girls
To youngsters
To children
To kids
To you guys

Gifts of thanks flowed onto Miss Smith's small desk. She received translations of the Beatrix Potter stories in Japanese, *Millions of Cats* in Dutch and *Alice in Wonderland* in Hebrew.

Then came the gift of all gifts. One visitor and one huge gift overwhelmed the entire community. This special gift surpassed all the others. It is a gift you can still see, study and share. The Spreading Tree of Miss Smith's Forest had reached across the world and now it was touching another tree in the Forest of Firsts, a tree that reached back in time.

CANADIAN CHILDREN'S LIBRARIANS COME TOGETHER
Before librarians across Canada formed their own association, Lillian initiated meetings of the children's librarians, joining them together in a Canadian association.

Number Six

The History Tree:
Past, Present and Future

The famous British illustrators in the late 1800s were Walter Crane, Kate Greenaway and Randolph Caldecott. Many children's book covers from this time were printed with beautiful designs and decorated with gold.

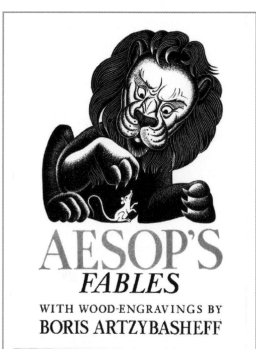

In 1934, as the County Librarian of Derbyshire, England, Edgar Osborne and his wife Mabel were invited to a conference in Toronto.

Edgar had toured hundreds of libraries in the U.S. and England, but he had never seen a library like Boys and Girls House. He admired the jungle mural and the map of fairyland, but he was overwhelmed by the fine collection, the trained librarians, the discussions and programs.

Miss Smith pulled out her silver tea set. As they sipped, she spoke about her children's books, using the word "literature" frequently. She told them about her Yardstick method of book selection. Her enthusiasm and dedication mirrored Edgar's own beliefs. He had never met anyone like Lillian Smith, who could discuss, in detail, all his favourite books.

Edgar Osborne, like Lillian Smith, had hungered for stories when he was young. As he grew older, he had started to collect books for children. As an adult, he owned rare and famous treasures which could no longer be found. The thousands of books in his collection included an early edition of *Aesop's Fables* and the original Goldilocks called *The Three Bears*.

ON GULLIVER'S TRAVELS

by Jonathan Swift

"It is interesting to speculate what he would have said in 1726 had someone told him that the book he worked on night after night in his big lonely house in Ireland would become the delight of many generations of boys and girls.

-Lillian Smith

Cover for *Gulliver's Travels* by Robin Jacques

Edgar had finally found someone who loved, valued and respected children's books as much as he did. If only his treasured collection could be here, under Miss Smith's care. She would know how to look after his special books. Edgar went home and rewrote his will, leaving his collection to Miss Smith. Then his wife Mabel died.

Thinking about honouring his wife's memory, Edgar said, "Perhaps I should give the collection to you now."

Moving two thousand priceless books over the ocean was a huge job. Luckily most of the books were small. The books were officially presented at Eaton's College Street store in Toronto on November 14, 1949. Each volume in the Osborne Collection has the inscription:

"This book forms part of the Osborne Collection of Children's Books, Presented to the Toronto Public Libraries by Edgar Osborne in Memory of his wife, Mabel Osborne."

Sheila Egoff, a librarian from Boys and Girls House, attended the opening celebration. Person after person said, "How lucky that this great collection has come to Toronto." Sheila remembered a line from Shakespeare: "Virtue…is not in our stars but in ourselves." She knew luck had nothing to do with it. The Toronto Public Library obtained the Osborne Collection because of one very special person named Lillian Smith.

The Forest of Firsts Was Complete

About thirty-five years after Miss Smith started to promote children's books, the rest of Canada finally followed. In 1946 the Canadian Association of Children's Librarians established the Book of the Year award for Canadian Children's literature. Then, in 1948 the Governor General's Literary Award Committee decided on an award in the field of children's writing.

In 1952, Lillian Smith reached age sixty-five, Canada's legal retirement age. The Forest of Firsts was complete. She had achieved her mission. Boys and Girls House operated smoothly. Specialized training existed for librarians. There were libraries in schools, in settlement houses and hospitals. She'd written a book listing good children's books. She had shared her love of these books with the world.

Every inch of her small office held memories. She sat for the last time at her desk as she crafted a good-bye letter. "Let us go forward," she addressed her librarians, "as we have always done, together." Then she went home.

Home was a house she shared with Margaret Johnston and Jean Thomson. Her housemates treated her royally, handling all the chores, the shopping, cooking and the gardening. Visitors, forming a kind of insiders group, made a permanent path from the library to this house. These librarians gathered for dinner and lively conversation. Always the talk was about books. Always Miss Smith's voice and opinions resonated.

Lillian Smith and her friend Jean Thompson

BOSS AND FRIEND

Lillian Smith's first "boss" ran the new Children's Rooms in New York. Anne Carroll Moore became Lillian's best friend. In letters addressed to Ann Caraway, a character from a book Anne wrote, Lillian confided private thoughts and feelings.

Anne Carroll Moore and Lillian Smith

Their most daunting visitor was her old friend, Anne Carroll Moore. She arrived with her overstuffed suitcase and beautiful handbags. "I've brought someone with me," she'd say, pulling a small wood doll from her bag. Her messy bag held no notebook, no pencil, calendar or date book, but Nicholas was always there.

Anne was a great critic and she had become an author too. One of her book characters was called Nicholas, and she gave the same name to her doll. Nicholas went to schools, library presentations and to Miss Smith's home for dinner. "You will never guess what happened to Nicholas on the way here," she'd say.

As the librarians discussed the book of the day, Nicholas had his say. Lillian respected Anne's opinions, even though they were presented through a doll.

Miss Smith often met with Anne in New York. Meetings for the Canadian Children's Library Association, a group she had founded, took her across Canada. The American Library Association still called on her as a former president and active supporter.

After one of these visits, Anne and Lillian were on their way to the airport in a taxi when Anne's favourite opera came

RETIREMENT

In 1952 , *The Globe and Mail,* Canada's national newspaper, printed, "For forty years, quietly and single-mindedly, this able woman has been developing the children's library services to (be) the best in the world."

on the radio. "Turn around," Anne commanded. No one seemed to mind missing the plane. They zoomed around Central Park, the trees swaying in time to the blaring music. They must have been as entranced as by one of their favourite tales.

Weekends Away

"My book and heart shall never part."

This is the quote that Lillian Smith placed at the front of her book *The Unreluctant Years*. Taken from a New England school book of the eighteenth century, the words appear opposite a wood engraving of a child reading.

The Shieling

LANDS OF PLEASURE

Books are keys to wisdom's treasure;
Books are gates to lands of pleasure
Books are paths that upward lead
Books are friends. Come, let us read.
  Inscription at the front of *Lands of*
  Pleasure, a book about Lillian Smith.

The three librarians found a perfect retreat just before Miss Smith retired. They purchased a cottage in Limestone, a small town near Toronto and dubbed it "The Shieling", a Scottish word for hut. Every weekend Margaret Johnston packed bags of food, and together with the dog, they drove to the country.

Here Miss Smith relaxed. With a martini drink or a glass of her favourite sherry by her side, she read and read. Then, responding to a request from the American Library Association, she outlined a book about children's books.

"A basic treatment of book selection for children...is...the only kind of book I would like to write...what I have for so long wanted to do," she said.

After her many years of planting the Forest of Firsts, she now set out to print her philosophies, the roots of everything she believed.

As dozens of daffodils bloomed around the Shieling, she wrote about the word "literature" and how it applies to children's books. She explained the Yardstick method of selection.

CLARENCE DAY AWARDS

In 1962, Lillian Smith became the first Canadian to receive this award. Given by the American Library Association, the award honoured *The Unreluctant Years* as a book of distinction which promoted a love of books and reading.

Lillian Smith's personal bookplate

Then she discussed in detail books in "which the imaginative content is greatest since these are more closely akin to pure literature."

A chapter each was devoted to rhymes, fairy tales, folklore, myths and epic heroes. She talked about picture books, fantasy books, historical fiction, poetry and biographies. She always connected her thoughts to the example set by the great classics. She always remembered the reader, the child.

Once published, *The Unreluctant Years* changed lives and attitudes. People interested in children's books savoured every thought. To this day the book remains an important reference for educators, parents and librarians. University courses placed it on their reading lists. More than one person made their way to Toronto to intern at Boys and Girls House after reading *The Unreluctant Years.* Even in her retirement, Lillian Smith remained a leader.

History
In the Making

THE OSBORNE COLLECTION

The Osborne Collection is a great collection of children's literature. Along with a handwritten copy of *Aesop's Fables* and an early picture book published in 1672, the collection has Florence Nightingale's childhood library, Queen Mary's books and material from famous families. Visitors come from all over the world.

The Osborne Collection Bookplate

In 1962, the Toronto Public Library Board agreed that the Osborne Collection should be extended. There were so many good children's books written since 1910. By the next century, they too would be history.

So 5,000 important children's books printed after 1910 were collected. Many of these titles were listed in Miss Smith's *Books for Boys and Girls.*

Naming this new collection was not difficult. By now, Lillian Smith's name was legendary in libraries. Every one agreed there was only one worthy name. The Lillian H. Smith Collection is now housed alongside the famous Osborne Collection.

Each year, new and wonderful books are added to this collection. Each one is put through the Lillian Smith test for a "good" book.

The End of a
New Beginning

GROWTH

Lillian Smith expanded children's services in Toronto to sixteen branches, thirty schools and two Settlement Houses.

Lillian Helena Smith's life story cannot be separated from the story of children's books. The adventure of her life, her beliefs about children, her work, and her personal relationships all centred around books.

In Canada today, the children's book industry has Miss Smith's indelible mark. She left us this Forest of Firsts, sprouting buds and branches of ideas and programs that permeate our libraries. She left us a book filled with her enduring philosophies.

Her life was books, children's books, and housed within them and the libraries she helped develop is the very spirit of Lillian Helena Smith.

Only now, nearly a century after she had the vision, are children's books receiving some of the attention she felt they deserved. Using her methods and guidelines, her followers search for another way to promote books to yet another child.

Legacy of an Indomitable Spirit

75 Years of Children's Services in the Toronto Public Library

An Exhibition from the Lillian H. Smith Collection

September 1—November 30, 1987

Prepared and described by Jill Shefrin and Dana Tenny

The Osborne & Lillian H. Smith Collections

Toronto Public Library

1987

A QUIET WOMAN

"Seldom has the wisdom and conviction of one quiet woman become a force that would affect the cultural life of children on five continents."

-Margaret Johnston

Of course life in any library has drastically changed. The numbers of books and members have skyrocketed. Behind the computerized efficiency, there is the memory of a woman who left her desk if a child needed help, a woman who knew every book on the shelves.

Next time you visit a library, find the children's section. Scan the shelves lined with hundreds of choices. Read the titles. Find a book that captivates you. Fly away with it to the imaginative world it creates.

Are you trembling at the scary parts? Are you laughing out loud at the funny lines? Can you "see" the characters? Are you bursting to tell your friends, "Read this book!"

Can you feel the magic?

Then the spirit of Lillian Helena Smith has touched you.

An early 20th century illustration of children playing "ring of roses".

The Lillian H. Smith branch of the Toronto Public Library on College Street in Toronto, which houses the Osborne Collection of Early Children's Books.

FOREVER

"The solid, sure foundation of good work is never lost. The best part of what we do endures."
-Lillian Smith

Chronology

1883   Toronto Public Library established.

1887   Lillian Helena Smith born in London, Ontario, Canada.

1905   Melvil Dewey introduces his Dewey Decimal System of classification.

1908   Dr. George H. Locke becomes Chief Librarian of the Toronto Public Library System. He introduces open shelves and card catalogues.

1909   Toronto Public Library reference library, funded by the Carnegie Foundation, opens at College and St. George Streets.

1910   Lillian Smith, one of the few women students, graduates from Victoria College, University of Toronto.

1910   Lillian Smith is one of 25 chosen students to train as a children's librarian at the The Carnegie Public Library in Pittsburgh.

1911   Anne Carroll Moore hires Lillian Smith for the Children's Division of the New York Public Library.

1912   Lillian Smith hired as Director of Children's Services for the Toronto Public Library

1913   Lillian Smith begins lecturing at the Ontario Department of Education.

1913   Lillian Smith establishes on-site training for children's librarians.

1914-1918   The First World War.

1915   Storytelling program is a great success.

1916   First issue of Ontario Library Review, a newsletter for library and book information, is published.

1917   Growing pains. "Would that we had a branch devoted entirely to boys and girls and the training of children's librarians."
            -Dr. George Locke

1918	The flu pandemic.
1921	Children are turned away from the library due to overcrowding.
1922	Boys and Girls House opens in a Victorian house at 40 St. George Street in Toronto.
1926	Lillian Smith opens the first school library in Toronto.
1927	Lillian Smith publishes the first edition of *Books for Boys and Girls*, a guide to quality children's books.
1928	Founding of the University of Toronto Library School. Lillian H. Smith lectures in children's literature and storytelling.
1928	Little Theatre and Story Hour Room added to Boys and Girls House.
1930	Introduction of Lillian Smith's own classification system designed for children's books.
1934	Lillian Smith provides assistance in the development of many Canadian children's libraries.
1934	English book collector Edgar Osborne visits Toronto.
1937	Mr. Charles R. Sanderson succeeds the late Dr. George H. Locke as Chief Librarian.
1949	Edgar Osborne donates the Osborne Collection to the Toronto Public Library.
1951	Boys and Girls House opens a new Children's Room and Theatre.
1952	Lillian Smith retires after forty years of distinguished service. Lillian Smith publishes her book, *The Unreluctant Years.*
1954	The third edition of *Books for Boys and Girls* edited by Miss Jean Thomson is published.
1962	The Lillian H. Smith Collection of children's books is established to mark the 50th anniversary of children's library service in Toronto.
1963	On April 22, farewell party for Boys and Girls House on St. George Street. The house is demolished in August 1963.
1964	Translation of *The Unreluctant Years* into Japanese.
1971	Translation of *The Unreluctant Years* into Italian.
1983	January 5, Lillian Helena Smith dies at age 95
1995	Boys and Girls House closes. The Collection is moved to a new library named the Lillian H. Smith Branch.

About the Author

Sydell Waxman's book *Changing the Pattern* (Napoleon 1996), the biography of Canada's first female physician Emily Stowe, won the Toronto Heritage Award of Merit in 1998. It was also awarded the Our Choice seal by the Canadian Children's Book Centre.

Her picture book *My Mannequins,* (©2000 by Napoleon), was an Our Choice selection and was chosen for a museum exhibit in Toronto. *The Rooster Prince* won a Storytelling World award of merit and was produced as a play at the Leah Posluns Theatre in Toronto.

Sydell's biography of Lillian H. Smith, *Believing in Books*, was honoured with the 2000 Frances E. Russell Award by IBBY (the International Board of Books for Young People) Canada for outstanding original research in children's literature.

Sydell lives in Thornhill, Ontario, with her husband Allan.

*To Julie, Kyle and Adlai, with loads of motherly love
and fond memories of sharing children's books.*

The author is grateful to those who opened their hearts and homes and shared their memories and thoughts. For their hospitality and generosity, special thanks to Sheila Egoff, Judith St. John, Margaret Johnston and Beatrice Johnston. To those who gave of their time and expertise in libraries and phone interviews, the author remains indebted to Dian Borek, Margery Fleming, Christina Steeles, Joyce Sowby, Ruth Osler, Leslie McGrath, Marion Cooke, Barbara Myrvold, Martha Scott, Ken Setterington, Robert Sink, John Stinson and Mary Shantz.

Sources of information included:
Personal interviews
The Toronto Public Library Archives housed in the Baldwin Room
The Archives of Boys and Girls House at the Osborne Collection
Lillian Smith's papers housed at the Osborne Collection
The Toronto Reference Library
New York Archives
City of Toronto Archives

For clarity, the experiences of many librarians and children have been integrated into the composite characters of Betty and Roger. The facts, the quotes and the scenarios remain historically accurate. "Only the names have been changed" to protect the innocent readers from confusion.

Photo and Art Credits

The following photo is from a book entitled *The Playford Ball* by Kate van Winkle Keller and Genevieve Shimer, published by CDSS, 1930: Page 56 (Country Dance and Song Society, Amherst, Massachusetts)

The following photos are from the personal collection of Margaret Johnston, the successor of Lillian Smith as head of Boys and Girls House: Pages 44, 68, 73, 76

The photo of Anne Carroll Moore on page 12 is from her biography by Francis Clarke Sayers, published by Atheneum in 1972

The following book covers are from the personal collection of Sydell Waxman: Pages 15 (*The Adventures of Pinocchio* by Carlo Collodi: The Children's Press, 1961), 43 (*Suprised by Joy* by C.S. Lewis: Harcourt, Brace and Co., 1955)

The illustration on page 80 is from the fruit crate label collection of Allan Waxman